# Landlocked Countries and Their Limitations

Copyright Page

TITLE: Landlocked Countries and Their Limitations

1<sup>ST</sup> Edition

Copyright @ 2023



ISBN: 9798223801641

Landlocked Countries and Their Unique Limitations

By Roberto Miguel Rodriguez

# Chapter 1: Landlocked countries: Focus on the specific challenges and limitations faced by countries surrounded by land.

Geographical constraints: Examining the impact of being landlocked on a country's access to international trade routes and resources.

In this subchapter, we delve into the unique challenges faced by landlocked countries due to their lack of direct access to international trade routes and resources. Being surrounded by land, these nations encounter various limitations that significantly impact their economies, diplomacy, and overall development.

Firstly, we explore the implications of limited access to trade routes on the economy and resource management of landlocked countries. Without direct access to ports or coastlines, these nations heavily rely on neighboring countries for trade and transportation of goods. This dependence often leads to higher transportation costs, delays, and trade barriers, hindering economic growth and development. We delve into the effects of resource scarcity and explore how landlocked countries can effectively manage and utilize their limited resources.

Next, we examine the unique foreign policy approaches adopted by landlocked countries to establish international cooperation and relations. Diplomatic strategies play a crucial role in overcoming the challenges of being landlocked. We explore how these nations engage in diplomatic negotiations, form alliances, and foster regional cooperation to improve their access to trade routes and resources.

Furthermore, we analyze the influence of landlocked countries on regional alliances, conflicts, and power dynamics. Despite their geographic limitations, landlocked nations can have a significant impact on regional geopolitics. We explore case studies and examine how these countries navigate regional dynamics, participate in alliances, and mitigate conflicts to safeguard their interests.

Transport infrastructure is another key aspect we investigate in this subchapter. We highlight the significance of efficient transportation systems, such as railways and pipelines, for landlocked countries' foreign policies. We discuss the importance of investing in infrastructure development and improving connectivity to overcome the challenges posed by geographical constraints.

Additionally, we address the increased vulnerability of landlocked countries to border conflicts and territorial disputes. Their lack of direct access to the sea makes them more susceptible to disputes with neighboring countries. We analyze the impact of these border conflicts on foreign policy decisions and explore strategies to navigate such challenges effectively.

Lastly, we explore the role of international organizations and agreements in assisting landlocked countries in overcoming their geographic constraints. We analyze the importance of multilateral cooperation and examine how international assistance and agreements can support these nations in improving their access to trade routes and resources.

Overall, this subchapter provides a comprehensive understanding of the unique limitations faced by landlocked countries and how these constraints impact their access to international trade routes and resources. It offers valuable insights for diplomats and policymakers in landlocked nations, shedding light on diplomatic strategies, regional dynamics, transport infrastructure, security concerns, and the role of international cooperation in overcoming these challenges.

Economic implications: Analyzing the economic challenges faced by landlocked countries, including limited market access, higher transportation costs, and reliance on neighboring countries for trade.

Landlocked countries face a unique set of economic challenges that significantly impact their development and foreign policy decisions. This subchapter delves into the economic implications of being landlocked, focusing on the limitations and constraints that these countries encounter.

One major challenge faced by landlocked countries is limited market access. Unlike coastal nations, these countries lack direct access to international markets, making it difficult for them to trade globally. This limitation restricts their ability to expand their export industries and diversify their economies. As a result, landlocked countries often rely heavily on their neighboring countries for trade, which can be both a blessing and a curse. While proximity to neighboring markets can provide opportunities for trade, it also exposes landlocked countries to potential trade restrictions and political disputes.

Another economic challenge for landlocked countries is higher transportation costs. Without direct access to ports, these countries must rely on transit routes through neighboring countries, increasing transportation costs significantly. The reliance on multiple modes of transportation, such as roads, railways, and pipelines, adds to the expenses and logistical complexities. These higher transportation costs make it challenging for landlocked countries to compete in global markets and can hinder their economic growth.

The economic implications of being landlocked also extend to resource management. Many landlocked countries possess valuable natural resources, such as minerals and energy reserves. However, limited access to trade routes restricts their ability to export these resources efficiently. This limitation not only affects their economic potential but also hampers their resource management capabilities. Landlocked countries must carefully navigate resource extraction and trade agreements with neighboring countries to maximize their economic benefits.

To overcome these economic challenges, landlocked countries adopt various diplomatic strategies. They establish international cooperation and relations to secure trade routes and transit agreements. This requires skillful negotiation and diplomatic engagement to ensure favorable trade conditions. Additionally, landlocked countries actively engage in regional alliances and organizations to influence regional dynamics, promote economic integration, and gain access to larger markets.

In conclusion, the economic implications of being landlocked are multifaceted and have a profound impact on the development and foreign policy decisions of these countries. Limited market access, higher transportation costs, and reliance on neighboring countries for trade pose significant challenges. However, landlocked countries can employ diplomatic strategies, develop efficient transport infrastructure, diversify trade partners, and seek assistance from international organizations to mitigate these challenges and enhance their economic potential. Understanding the economic implications of landlockedness is crucial for diplomats and policymakers working with landlocked countries to address their unique limitations and promote their sustainable development.

Infrastructure development: Investigating the importance of developing efficient transport systems, such as railways and pipelines, to overcome the limitations of being landlocked.

Infrastructure development plays a crucial role in overcoming the limitations faced by landlocked countries. Efficient transport systems, such as railways and pipelines, are particularly important in enabling these nations to connect with global markets and overcome the challenges posed by their geographic constraints. This subchapter will delve into the significance of developing such infrastructure and its impact on the foreign policies of landlocked countries.

One of the key challenges faced by landlocked countries is limited access to trade routes, which hampers their ability to engage in international trade and commerce. Efficient transport systems, such as railways and pipelines, provide a viable alternative to overcome this limitation. These infrastructure projects not only facilitate the movement of goods and resources but also enhance connectivity and integration with neighboring countries and international markets.

By investing in railways, landlocked countries can establish vital trade corridors that connect them to ports and coastal regions. This enables them to transport goods more efficiently, reducing costs and transit times. Similarly, the development of pipelines allows for the efficient transportation of resources, such as oil and gas, from landlocked regions to international markets.

The establishment of efficient transport systems has a direct impact on the foreign policies of landlocked countries. It enhances their bargaining power in negotiating transit agreements with neighboring countries, ensuring smooth and uninterrupted movement of goods. Additionally, it enables landlocked nations to diversify their trade partners, reducing their dependence on neighboring countries and mitigating the risks associated with geopolitical tensions or border disputes.

Furthermore, the development of transport infrastructure can also contribute to regional dynamics and geopolitics. Landlocked countries that successfully develop efficient transportation systems can become important hubs for regional trade and connectivity. This enhances their influence in regional alliances, power dynamics, and conflict resolution.

To achieve these objectives, landlocked countries often adopt unique foreign policy approaches. They seek to establish international cooperation and relations, particularly with transit countries and regional powers, to secure favorable transit agreements and ensure the smooth movement of goods.

In conclusion, the importance of developing efficient transport systems, such as railways and pipelines, cannot be overstated for landlocked countries. Infrastructure development plays a pivotal role in overcoming the limitations imposed by their geographic constraints. It enables these nations to connect with global markets, diversify their trade partners, enhance regional connectivity, and shape their foreign policies. Therefore, investing in transport infrastructure is vital for landlocked countries to navigate the challenges they face and unlock their economic potential.

# Chapter 2: Resource dependence: Analyzing the impact of limited access to trade routes and its effects on the economy and resource management.

Challenges in resource extraction: Assessing the difficulties faced by landlocked countries in accessing and exporting their natural resources.

Resource extraction plays a crucial role in the economic development of any nation. However, for landlocked countries, the task becomes significantly more challenging due to their lack of direct access to the sea. This subchapter aims to shed light on the unique limitations and difficulties faced by landlocked countries in accessing and exporting their natural resources.

One of the primary challenges faced by landlocked countries is limited access to trade routes. Without direct access to the sea, these countries heavily rely on neighboring nations for transit, making them vulnerable to disruptions in transportation infrastructure and trade routes. This limited access can have a profound impact on the economy and resource management of landlocked countries, leading to increased costs, delays, and inefficiencies in resource extraction and export.

To overcome these challenges, landlocked countries have adopted unique foreign policy approaches. Diplomatic strategies are crucial in establishing international cooperation and relations to ensure access to trade routes. By engaging in diplomatic negotiations and forging alliances, landlocked countries strive to secure transit agreements and gain preferential treatment from neighboring coastal nations.

Moreover, the geopolitical dynamics of a region can significantly influence the challenges faced by landlocked countries. These nations often find themselves at the center of regional alliances, conflicts, and power dynamics. Their limited access to resources can make them both a target and a bargaining chip in these dynamics, necessitating careful navigation of diplomatic relations to protect their interests.

Efficient transportation systems, such as railways and pipelines, are of paramount importance for landlocked countries. Developing and maintaining robust transport infrastructure becomes a critical component of their foreign policies. By investing in transportation networks, landlocked countries aim to enhance their connectivity and reduce dependence on neighboring countries for trade.

Border conflicts and territorial disputes pose additional challenges for landlocked countries. Their increased vulnerability to such disputes can significantly impact foreign policy decisions, as these nations must carefully navigate the complexities of border issues while ensuring resource extraction and export.

Multilateral cooperation and international organizations play a vital role in assisting landlocked countries in overcoming their geographic constraints. Through agreements and partnerships, these organizations provide crucial support in improving transportation infrastructure, enhancing trade facilitation, and mitigating the challenges faced by landlocked nations.

Trade diversification is another strategy employed by landlocked countries to reduce their dependence on neighboring countries. By expanding their trade partners and diversifying their export destinations, these nations can mitigate the risks associated with limited access to trade routes.

Security challenges also loom large for landlocked countries. Their geographic constraints make them susceptible to various security concerns, including smuggling, piracy, and terrorism. These challenges influence foreign policy decisions, as landlocked countries must prioritize security measures to protect their resources and maintain stability.

Lastly, development aid and assistance play a crucial role in supporting landlocked countries' development efforts and enhancing their foreign policy capabilities. By receiving foreign aid, these nations can invest in infrastructure development, technological advancements, and capacity building, ultimately improving their resource extraction and export capabilities.

In conclusion, landlocked countries face a myriad of challenges in accessing and exporting their natural resources. From limited access to trade routes and transportation infrastructure to geopolitical dynamics and security concerns, these nations must navigate a complex landscape to ensure their economic development and resource management. Through diplomatic strategies, multilateral cooperation, trade diversification, and development aid, landlocked countries strive to overcome these challenges and establish themselves as active players in the global economy.

Resource management strategies: Exploring the approaches adopted by landlocked countries to effectively manage their limited resources and ensure sustainable development.

Resource management strategies are crucial for landlocked countries, which face unique challenges in effectively managing their limited resources and ensuring sustainable development. These countries, surrounded by land and lacking direct access to the sea, must adopt specific approaches to overcome their limitations and promote economic growth.

Limited access to trade routes is a major obstacle faced by landlocked countries. The reliance on neighboring countries for transit and trade increases the vulnerability of their economies and resource management. To address this challenge, landlocked countries often focus on diplomatic strategies to establish international cooperation and relations. By building strong diplomatic ties, these countries can negotiate transit agreements and secure alternative trade routes, reducing their dependence on a single access point.

Geopolitics and regional dynamics play a crucial role in shaping the foreign policies of landlocked countries. These countries can influence regional alliances, conflicts, and power dynamics, leveraging their geographic location to foster cooperation and stability. By actively engaging in regional initiatives and promoting dialogue, landlocked countries can enhance their position on the global stage and secure their resource management interests.

Efficient transportation infrastructure, such as railways and pipelines, is vital for landlocked countries' foreign policies. Developing and maintaining a robust transportation network enables these countries to efficiently transport goods and resources, reducing trade barriers and enhancing their competitiveness. By investing in transport infrastructure, landlocked countries can attract foreign investments and diversify their trade partners, reducing their dependence on neighboring countries.

Border conflicts and territorial disputes pose a significant challenge for landlocked countries. The vulnerability of their borders increases the risk of disputes and conflicts, which can have severe implications for resource management and foreign policy decisions. Landlocked countries must adopt diplomatic strategies to address border disputes, promoting dialogue and peaceful resolutions to safeguard their resources and promote regional stability.

Multilateral cooperation plays a crucial role in assisting landlocked countries in overcoming their geographic constraints. International organizations and agreements provide platforms for dialogue, assistance, and knowledge sharing, enabling landlocked countries to access resources, technology, and expertise. By actively engaging in multilateral cooperation, landlocked countries can enhance their resource management capabilities and promote sustainable development.

Trade diversification is another essential strategy employed by landlocked countries. By expanding their trade partners and reducing dependence on neighboring countries, landlocked nations can mitigate the risks associated with limited access to trade routes. Through trade diversification, these countries can access new markets, attract foreign investments, and promote economic growth.

Security challenges are a significant concern for landlocked countries. Their geographic location makes them more susceptible to security threats, including transnational crime, terrorism, and political instability. Addressing these challenges is crucial for effective resource management and foreign policy decisions. Landlocked countries must prioritize security cooperation, engage in regional security initiatives, and seek assistance from international partners to enhance their security capabilities.

Development aid and assistance play a vital role in supporting landlocked countries' development efforts and enhancing their foreign policy capabilities. Foreign aid can provide financial resources, technical expertise, and capacity building to address the unique challenges faced by landlocked countries. By leveraging development assistance, these countries can improve their resource management strategies, promote sustainable development, and enhance their global standing.

In conclusion, landlocked countries face specific challenges and limitations that require tailored resource management strategies. By exploring approaches such as diplomatic strategies, efficient transportation infrastructure, multilateral cooperation, trade diversification, and development aid, these countries can effectively manage their limited resources and ensure sustainable development. Understanding the unique circumstances of landlocked countries is crucial for diplomats and policymakers to address their needs and support their efforts towards economic growth and prosperity.

Chapter 3: Diplomatic strategies: Examining the unique foreign policy approaches adopted by landlocked countries to establish international cooperation and relations.

Bilateral agreements: Analyzing the importance of diplomatic negotiations and agreements with neighboring countries for landlocked countries' trade and transportation access.

Landlocked countries face unique challenges when it comes to trade and transportation access due to their lack of direct access to the sea. These countries heavily rely on their neighboring countries to facilitate the movement of goods and people, making bilateral agreements crucial for their economic development and stability.

Diplomatic negotiations and agreements play a vital role in ensuring that landlocked countries have reliable and efficient trade routes. By establishing diplomatic relations with their neighboring countries, landlocked nations can negotiate transit agreements that grant them access to ports and transport networks. These agreements outline the rights and responsibilities of both parties and provide a legal framework for the movement of goods and people across borders.

For landlocked countries, these bilateral agreements are not just about trade and transportation; they are also about fostering good relations and building trust with their neighbors. Diplomatic negotiations provide an opportunity for landlocked nations to address any concerns or disputes that may arise and to find mutually beneficial solutions. By engaging in diplomatic dialogue, landlocked countries can build strong relationships with their neighbors, which can lead to increased cooperation in various areas, including trade, security, and regional development.

Furthermore, bilateral agreements help landlocked countries diversify their trade partners and reduce dependence on a single route or country. By negotiating agreements with multiple neighboring countries, landlocked nations can ensure that their trade routes are not solely reliant on one country's goodwill or political stability. This diversification of trade partners enhances the resilience of landlocked countries' economies and reduces the risk of disruptions caused by geopolitical tensions or conflicts.

In conclusion, the importance of diplomatic negotiations and agreements with neighboring countries for landlocked countries' trade and transportation access cannot be overstated. These bilateral agreements provide a foundation for economic growth, stability, and regional cooperation. By engaging in diplomatic dialogue and forging strong relationships with their neighbors, landlocked nations can ensure reliable and efficient trade routes, diversify their trade partners, and strengthen their overall foreign policy capabilities.

Regional cooperation: Expanding on the role of landlocked countries in regional alliances and organizations to enhance their diplomatic influence and overcome geographic limitations.

Regional cooperation plays a crucial role in enhancing the diplomatic influence of landlocked countries and overcoming their geographic limitations. In a world where connectivity and interdependence are increasingly important, landlocked countries have unique challenges that require innovative solutions. This subchapter explores the ways in which landlocked countries can expand their role in regional alliances and organizations to overcome their limitations and increase their diplomatic influence.

Landlocked countries face numerous obstacles due to their lack of direct access to the sea. These limitations can hinder their economic growth, trade, and overall development. However, by actively participating in regional alliances and organizations, landlocked countries can leverage their geographic position to enhance their diplomatic influence.

One key aspect of regional cooperation is the development of transportation infrastructure. Landlocked countries can collaborate with their neighboring coastal countries to improve road, rail, and air transportation networks. By investing in these infrastructure projects, landlocked countries can establish efficient trade corridors, reducing transit times and costs. This not only boosts their own economies but also enhances their influence within the region.

Regional alliances and organizations also provide landlocked countries with platforms to voice their concerns and contribute to decision-making processes. By actively engaging in diplomatic discussions and negotiations, landlocked countries can ensure that their specific needs and challenges are taken into account. This enables them to shape regional policies and initiatives that cater to their unique circumstances.

Furthermore, regional alliances and organizations offer landlocked countries opportunities for cooperation in areas such as energy, water resources, and security. By pooling resources, sharing knowledge, and coordinating efforts, landlocked countries can address common challenges and achieve mutually beneficial outcomes. This fosters regional stability and strengthens diplomatic ties among participating countries.

In conclusion, regional cooperation is crucial for landlocked countries to overcome their geographic limitations and enhance their diplomatic influence. By actively participating in regional alliances and organizations, landlocked countries can improve transportation infrastructure, voice their concerns, contribute to decision-making processes, and cooperate on various issues. Through these efforts, landlocked countries can effectively navigate the challenges they face, strengthen their foreign policies, and play a more significant role in the global arena.

# Chapter 4: Geopolitics and regional dynamics: Exploring the influence of landlocked countries on regional alliances, conflicts, and power dynamics.

Impact on regional alliances: Assessing how landlocked countries navigate regional alliances and contribute to regional stability and development.

Impact on Regional Alliances: Assessing How Landlocked Countries Navigate Regional Alliances and Contribute to Regional Stability and Development

Landlocked countries face a unique set of challenges and limitations due to their geographical location. These nations are surrounded by land, making access to trade routes and international markets more difficult. As a result, landlocked countries often have to navigate regional alliances and establish diplomatic strategies to overcome these limitations and contribute to regional stability and development.

One key aspect to consider is the impact of limited access to trade routes on the economy and resource management of landlocked countries. Without direct access to ports and sea routes, these nations heavily rely on their neighbors for trade and transportation. This dependence can have both positive and negative consequences, as it can foster economic cooperation and regional integration, but it can also make landlocked countries vulnerable to trade disruptions and resource conflicts.

To address these challenges, landlocked countries adopt unique foreign policy approaches and establish international cooperation and relations. Diplomatic strategies play a vital role in mitigating the limitations imposed by landlocked status. These countries actively engage in regional alliances and organizations to enhance their diplomatic capabilities and influence on regional dynamics and conflicts.

Moreover, the significance of efficient transportation systems, such as railways and pipelines, cannot be overstated for landlocked countries' foreign policies. Developing and maintaining a robust transport infrastructure is crucial for ensuring smooth trade flows and accessing global markets. Landlocked countries strategically invest in improving their transportation networks and establishing connections with neighboring countries to enhance their trade capabilities and strengthen their position in regional alliances.

However, landlocked countries also face increased vulnerability to border conflicts and territorial disputes. The limited access to international waters makes them more susceptible to disputes over transit routes and border control. Consequently, these countries must carefully navigate these conflicts and make foreign policy decisions that prioritize regional stability and cooperation.

Multilateral cooperation and international organizations play a crucial role in assisting landlocked countries in overcoming their geographic constraints. By providing support, aid, and promoting trade facilitation measures, these organizations help landlocked nations diversify their trade partners and reduce dependence on neighboring countries.

Furthermore, landlocked countries face unique security challenges that influence their foreign policy decisions. These nations often have to prioritize security concerns related to smuggling, terrorism, and illicit activities. Consequently, their foreign policies emphasize the importance of regional stability and cooperation to tackle these security challenges effectively.

Lastly, development aid and assistance play a vital role in supporting landlocked countries' development efforts and enhancing their foreign policy capabilities. International aid helps these nations invest in infrastructure, education, and healthcare, enabling them to overcome the limitations imposed by their landlocked status and contribute to regional stability and development.

In conclusion, landlocked countries face a myriad of challenges and limitations due to their geographical location. However, through strategic diplomatic approaches, efficient transportation infrastructure, and regional cooperation, these nations can navigate regional alliances and contribute to regional stability and development. International organizations, trade diversification, and development aid also play a crucial role in assisting landlocked countries in overcoming their unique constraints and enhancing their foreign policy capabilities.

Conflict vulnerability: Examining the increased vulnerability of landlocked countries to border conflicts and territorial disputes and their impact on foreign policy decisions.

The subchapter titled "Conflict vulnerability" delves into the heightened susceptibility of landlocked countries to border conflicts and territorial disputes, and the consequential impact on their foreign policy decisions. This chapter sheds light on the unique challenges faced by landlocked nations and aims to provide diplomats and individuals interested in international relations with a comprehensive understanding of this complex issue.

Landlocked countries, by virtue of their geographical location, face inherent limitations and vulnerabilities. Their lack of direct access to the sea makes them heavily reliant on neighboring countries for trade routes and transportation networks. This dependence on transit countries exposes them to heightened risks of border disputes and conflicts, as well as potential disruptions to their trade and economy. Moreover, their limited territorial boundaries can result in territorial disputes with neighboring states, further exacerbating their vulnerability.

The subchapter highlights the impact of these conflicts and disputes on the foreign policy decisions of landlocked countries. It explores how these nations navigate diplomatic strategies to mitigate tensions, establish international cooperation, and maintain peaceful relations with their neighbors. By analyzing case studies and diplomatic approaches adopted by various landlocked countries, diplomats can gain insights into effective conflict resolution and preventive measures.

Furthermore, the subchapter examines the role of regional dynamics and geopolitics in shaping the vulnerability of landlocked countries to conflicts. It explores how their unique position influences regional alliances, power dynamics, and the potential for spillover effects from neighboring conflicts. By understanding these dynamics, diplomats can formulate informed policies and strategies to mitigate the risks and protect the interests of landlocked nations.

Additionally, the subchapter delves into the significance of efficient transport infrastructure, such as railways and pipelines, for landlocked countries' foreign policies. It emphasizes the need for investment in transportation networks to enhance connectivity and reduce dependence on transit countries. By improving their transport infrastructure, landlocked countries can strengthen their negotiating power and diversify their trade partners, reducing their vulnerability to conflicts and disputes.

In conclusion, the subchapter on conflict vulnerability provides diplomats with a comprehensive analysis of the unique challenges faced by landlocked countries in relation to border conflicts and territorial disputes. By examining the impact of these challenges on foreign policy decisions, diplomats can better understand the complexities associated with landlocked nations and work towards effective conflict resolution and cooperation.

Chapter 5: Transport infrastructure: Investigating the significance of efficient transportation systems, such as railways and pipelines, for landlocked countries' foreign policies.

Importance of transportation networks: Exploring how well-developed transport infrastructure can enhance a landlocked country's connectivity and trade opportunities.

Importance of Transportation Networks: Exploring how well-developed transport infrastructure can enhance a landlocked country's connectivity and trade opportunities

Transportation networks play a crucial role in shaping the economic and geopolitical landscape of landlocked countries. These nations, surrounded by land with limited access to sea routes, face unique challenges in terms of connectivity and trade opportunities. In this subchapter, we will delve into the significance of efficient transportation systems and how they can enhance a landlocked country's foreign policies and economic growth.

For landlocked countries, the development of transport infrastructure, such as railways, pipelines, and road networks, is vital for connecting with neighboring countries and global markets. Efficient transportation systems provide these countries with the means to overcome geographical constraints and establish trade links. By investing in and expanding their transportation networks, landlocked nations can significantly improve their connectivity, reducing the cost and time required to transport goods and services.

Enhanced connectivity through well-developed transport infrastructure not only facilitates trade but also attracts foreign direct investment (FDI). Investors are more likely to consider landlocked countries as viable investment destinations when they have reliable and efficient transportation networks. Moreover, improved connectivity can lead to job creation, increased economic activity, and improved living standards for the population.

Additionally, a well-connected landlocked country gains strategic advantages in regional alliances, conflicts, and power dynamics. By strengthening their transportation networks, landlocked nations can enhance their geopolitical influence and establish themselves as key players in regional trade and cooperation. These countries can leverage their geographical location to become transit hubs, facilitating trade routes between neighboring countries and acting as a bridge between different regions.

Furthermore, the development of transport infrastructure can help landlocked countries diversify their trade partners and reduce their dependence on neighboring countries. Limited access to trade routes often leads to overreliance on a few neighboring countries for imports and exports. By investing in transportation networks that connect to multiple borders, landlocked nations can expand their trade horizons, tapping into new markets and reducing their vulnerability to external shocks.

In conclusion, a well-developed transport infrastructure is instrumental in enhancing a landlocked country's connectivity and trade opportunities. Efficient transportation systems allow these nations to overcome geographical limitations, attract foreign investment, and improve their geopolitical influence. By investing in their transportation networks, landlocked countries can diversify their trade partners, reduce dependence on neighboring countries, and accelerate their economic growth.

Investment in infrastructure: Analyzing the role of foreign investment and international cooperation in supporting the development of transport infrastructure in landlocked countries.

Introduction:

The development of efficient transport infrastructure is crucial for landlocked countries to overcome their geographical limitations and integrate into the global economy. This subchapter explores the role of foreign investment and international cooperation in supporting the development of transport infrastructure in landlocked countries. It delves into the challenges faced by these countries and highlights the significance of efficient transportation systems for their foreign policies.

Importance of transport infrastructure for landlocked countries' foreign policies:

Transport infrastructure plays a pivotal role in landlocked countries' foreign policies. Efficient railways, pipelines, and roads connect them to neighboring countries and international trade routes, enabling the movement of goods, services, and people. This connectivity enhances their economic competitiveness, facilitates trade diversification, and reduces dependence on neighboring countries.

Foreign investment and international cooperation:

Foreign investment and international cooperation are instrumental in supporting the development of transport infrastructure in landlocked countries. For instance, foreign direct investment (FDI) can provide the necessary capital and expertise for infrastructure projects. International cooperation through bilateral and multilateral agreements can also facilitate the transfer of technology, knowledge sharing, and capacity building in the transport sector.

Challenges and limitations:

Landlocked countries face unique challenges and limitations in developing their transport infrastructure. Limited access to maritime trade routes, geographical barriers, and political instability can hinder infrastructure development. Additionally, financial constraints and inadequate institutional capacity pose significant obstacles.

The role of international organizations and agreements:

International organizations and agreements play a crucial role in assisting landlocked countries in overcoming their geographic constraints. Organizations such as the United Nations Conference on Trade and Development (UNCTAD) and the World Bank provide technical assistance, financial support, and policy advice. Agreements like the United Nations Convention on the Law of the Sea (UNCLOS) and regional initiatives promote cooperation and address the specific needs of landlocked countries.

Foreign aid and assistance:

Development aid and assistance from foreign countries also contribute to supporting landlocked countries' development efforts and enhancing their foreign policy capabilities. Aid programs can focus on infrastructure development, capacity building, and promoting trade diversification. Donor countries can also provide technical expertise and knowledge transfer to strengthen the transport sector.

Conclusion:

Investment in transport infrastructure is essential for landlocked countries to overcome their unique limitations and achieve sustainable development. Foreign investment, international cooperation, and development aid play vital roles in supporting the development of efficient transportation systems. Through strategic partnerships and multilateral agreements, landlocked countries can improve their connectivity, enhance trade diversification, and strengthen their foreign policy capabilities.

Chapter 6: Border conflicts and territorial disputes: Studying the increased vulnerability of landlocked countries to border disputes and their impact on foreign policy decisions.

Border disputes and security concerns: Assessing the unique security challenges faced by landlocked countries due to their geographical position and territorial disputes.

Landlocked countries face numerous security challenges as a result of their geographical position and territorial disputes. These challenges, which often have far-reaching consequences, are of great concern to diplomats and policymakers. Understanding and addressing these security concerns is crucial for ensuring stability and promoting international cooperation.

One major security challenge faced by landlocked countries is the vulnerability to border disputes. With no direct access to maritime trade routes, landlocked countries heavily rely on their neighboring countries for transit, making them more susceptible to conflicts over borders and territorial claims. These disputes can escalate into full-blown conflicts, disrupting trade, and causing political instability. Diplomats must carefully navigate these issues, employing diplomatic strategies to prevent and resolve border disputes through dialogue and negotiations.

Furthermore, the lack of direct access to the sea poses significant security risks for landlocked countries. Traditional security threats such as terrorism, arms smuggling, and organized crime can be exacerbated due to the absence of maritime borders. Diplomatic efforts should focus on establishing international cooperation and collaboration to enhance security measures, intelligence sharing, and counter-terrorism initiatives.

Landlocked countries are also heavily dependent on their transport infrastructure for their economic development and foreign policy decisions. Efficient transportation systems, such as railways and pipelines, are crucial for trade and connectivity. Diplomats must advocate for investments in transport infrastructure and work towards establishing regional alliances and agreements to enhance connectivity and trade routes.

Multilateral cooperation plays a vital role in assisting landlocked countries in overcoming their geographic constraints. International organizations and agreements provide platforms for dialogue and negotiation, facilitating the resolution of border disputes and promoting regional stability. Diplomats need to actively engage with these organizations and leverage their resources to address security challenges faced by landlocked countries effectively.

To reduce their dependence on neighboring countries, landlocked countries must diversify their trade partners. Diplomats play a key role in promoting trade diversification strategies and fostering economic cooperation with countries outside the region. This not only enhances economic resilience but also reduces the vulnerability of landlocked countries to political and economic pressures from neighboring countries.

Lastly, development aid and assistance are critical for supporting landlocked countries' development efforts and enhancing their foreign policy capabilities. Diplomats should actively engage with donor countries and international financial institutions to secure assistance and investments in key sectors such as infrastructure, education, healthcare, and technology.

In conclusion, landlocked countries face unique security challenges due to their geographical position and territorial disputes. Diplomats must navigate these challenges by focusing on border disputes, enhancing security measures, improving transport infrastructure, fostering multilateral cooperation, diversifying trade partners, and securing development aid. By addressing these security concerns effectively, landlocked countries can overcome their limitations and promote stability, economic growth, and international cooperation.

Diplomatic resolutions: Investigating the diplomatic strategies employed by landlocked countries to resolve border conflicts and maintain peaceful relations with neighboring countries.

In this subchapter, we will delve into the intricate world of diplomatic resolutions and the strategies employed by landlocked countries to resolve border conflicts and maintain peaceful relations with their neighboring countries. Landlocked countries face unique challenges due to their geographical limitations, which often make them more susceptible to border disputes and conflicts with neighboring nations. However, through diplomatic approaches, these nations have been able to navigate the complexities and establish cooperative relationships.

One of the key diplomatic strategies employed by landlocked countries is a commitment to peaceful negotiations and dialogue. These nations understand the importance of maintaining stability and avoiding conflicts that could disrupt trade routes and jeopardize their economic development. By engaging in diplomatic talks, they can address border disputes and territorial claims in a peaceful and mutually beneficial manner.

Another diplomatic approach embraced by landlocked countries is the active participation in regional alliances and organizations. By joining forces with neighboring nations and participating in regional initiatives, landlocked countries can foster cooperation and build trust. These alliances provide a platform for dialogue, conflict resolution, and the establishment of common goals that benefit all parties involved.

Landlocked countries also recognize the significance of transport infrastructure in their foreign policy decisions. Efficient transportation systems, such as railways and pipelines, are crucial for these nations to maintain connectivity with global markets. Thus, diplomatic efforts are often directed towards securing agreements and partnerships that ensure the smooth flow of goods and resources through neighboring countries.

Furthermore, landlocked countries have embraced multilateral cooperation as a means to overcome their geographic constraints. International organizations and agreements play a vital role in assisting these nations in addressing their unique challenges. Through these platforms, landlocked countries can gain access to development aid, technical assistance, and expertise that can enhance their foreign policy capabilities and support their economic growth.

Additionally, landlocked countries understand the importance of trade diversification to reduce their dependence on neighboring countries. By pursuing trade agreements with a diverse range of partners, these nations can mitigate the risks associated with limited access to trade routes and foster economic resilience.

Lastly, security concerns are a central aspect of landlocked countries' foreign policy decisions. These nations face unique security challenges due to their lack of direct access to the sea. Therefore, diplomatic efforts are often focused on building strong relationships with neighboring countries and engaging in cooperative security arrangements to ensure regional stability.

In conclusion, landlocked countries employ various diplomatic strategies to resolve border conflicts and maintain peaceful relations with neighboring nations. By prioritizing peaceful negotiations, engaging in regional alliances, investing in transport infrastructure, embracing multilateral cooperation, diversifying trade partners, and addressing security concerns, these nations can navigate the challenges posed by their geographical limitations and establish prosperous relationships with their neighbors.

Chapter 7: Multilateral cooperation: Analyzing the role of international organizations and agreements in assisting landlocked countries in overcoming their geographic constraints.

Engagement with international organizations: Examining how landlocked countries leverage their membership in international organizations to advocate for their interests and enhance their diplomatic capabilities.

Landlocked countries face a unique set of challenges and limitations due to their geographic location, being surrounded by land and lacking direct access to the sea. These countries often struggle with limited trade routes, resource dependence, border conflicts, and security concerns. In order to overcome these obstacles and strengthen their diplomatic capabilities, landlocked countries have increasingly turned to international organizations for support and cooperation.

Membership in international organizations provides landlocked countries with a platform to advocate for their interests on the global stage. These organizations offer a forum for diplomatic engagement, enabling landlocked countries to establish relationships with other nations and foster international cooperation. Through their membership, landlocked countries can raise awareness about the specific challenges they face and promote policies that address their unique limitations.

International organizations also play a crucial role in assisting landlocked countries in overcoming their geographic constraints. These organizations provide technical assistance, capacity building, and financial support to help landlocked countries improve their transportation infrastructure, such as railways and pipelines. By enhancing their transport networks, landlocked countries can improve their connectivity and reduce their dependency on neighboring countries for trade.

Furthermore, international organizations facilitate trade diversification for landlocked countries. Through trade agreements and partnerships, these organizations help landlocked countries expand their markets and reduce their reliance on a limited number of neighboring countries. By diversifying their trade partners, landlocked countries can enhance their economic resilience and reduce vulnerability to disruptions in regional dynamics.

Additionally, international organizations contribute to the security of landlocked countries. They provide platforms for dialogue and conflict resolution, assisting landlocked countries in resolving border disputes and territorial conflicts. By promoting peace and stability in the region, international organizations help landlocked countries mitigate security concerns and shape their foreign policy decisions.

Moreover, international organizations offer development aid and assistance to landlocked countries, supporting their efforts to overcome infrastructure gaps, improve resource management, and enhance their foreign policy capabilities. Through these development programs, landlocked countries can strengthen their economies and improve the well-being of their citizens.

In conclusion, engagement with international organizations is vital for landlocked countries to overcome their unique challenges and limitations. Membership in these organizations allows landlocked countries to advocate for their interests, enhance their diplomatic capabilities, and seek support for improving transport infrastructure, diversifying trade, resolving border conflicts, and addressing security concerns. By leveraging their membership, landlocked countries can navigate the challenges they face and achieve greater economic prosperity and diplomatic influence on the global stage.

Benefits of multilateral agreements: Exploring the advantages of participating in regional and global agreements for landlocked countries, such as improved trade facilitation and access to development aid.

Benefits of Multilateral Agreements: Exploring the Advantages of Participating in Regional and Global Agreements for Landlocked Countries

Landlocked countries face a unique set of challenges due to their lack of direct access to coastal areas and international trade routes. These countries, surrounded by land, often struggle with limited transportation options, reliance on neighboring countries for trade, and increased vulnerability to border disputes. However, participating in multilateral agreements at both regional and global levels can offer a range of benefits for these nations, including improved trade facilitation and access to development aid. In this subchapter, we will delve into the advantages that landlocked countries can gain from engaging in such agreements.

One of the primary advantages of multilateral agreements for landlocked countries is enhanced trade facilitation. These agreements provide a framework for reducing trade barriers, streamlining customs procedures, and harmonizing regulations. By participating in these agreements, landlocked countries can benefit from improved access to international markets, which can boost their economies and promote sustainable development. Additionally, these agreements often include provisions for transit rights and preferential treatment for landlocked countries, further facilitating their trade activities.

Participation in multilateral agreements also enables landlocked countries to access development aid and assistance. International organizations and donor countries often prioritize supporting landlocked nations due to their unique challenges. Through these agreements, landlocked countries can tap into financial resources, technical expertise, and capacity-building programs that can help them overcome their limitations and drive socio-economic growth. Development aid can also enhance landlocked countries' foreign policy capabilities, enabling them to engage more effectively on the global stage and establish diplomatic relations with a broader range of countries.

Moreover, multilateral agreements offer landlocked countries a platform to diversify their trade partners beyond their immediate neighbors. By reducing dependence on neighboring countries, landlocked nations can mitigate the risks associated with geopolitical tensions and border disputes. This diversification of trade partners can also lead to increased economic resilience and stability.

In conclusion, participating in regional and global multilateral agreements brings numerous benefits for landlocked countries. These agreements offer improved trade facilitation, access to development aid, and opportunities for trade diversification. By engaging in such agreements, landlocked nations can overcome their unique limitations and establish themselves as active players in the global economy. It is crucial for diplomats, policymakers, and stakeholders to recognize the significance of multilateral cooperation in assisting landlocked countries and supporting their development efforts.

Chapter 8: Trade diversification: Examining the strategies employed by landlocked countries to diversify their trade partners and reduce dependence on neighboring countries.

Trade policy reforms: Analyzing the policy measures adopted by landlocked countries to attract foreign investment, promote export diversification, and reduce trade barriers.

Trade policy reforms play a crucial role in the development and growth of landlocked countries. These nations, surrounded by land and lacking direct access to trade routes, face unique challenges and limitations that require specific policy measures to attract foreign investment, promote export diversification, and reduce trade barriers. In this subchapter, we will analyze the policy measures adopted by landlocked countries to overcome these challenges and enhance their foreign policy capabilities.

One of the key strategies employed by landlocked countries is to attract foreign investment. Recognizing the importance of foreign capital for economic development, these nations have implemented policies to create a favorable investment climate. This includes establishing special economic zones, offering tax incentives, and streamlining bureaucratic processes. By attracting foreign investment, landlocked countries can enhance their infrastructure, develop industries, and create employment opportunities.

Another important aspect is promoting export diversification. Landlocked countries often face limited export options due to their geographic constraints. To overcome this, they adopt policies to support the development of non-traditional industries and products. This includes providing financial incentives, investing in research and development, and facilitating market access. By diversifying their exports, landlocked countries can reduce their dependence on neighboring countries and enhance their competitiveness in the global market.

Reducing trade barriers is also crucial for landlocked countries. With limited access to trade routes, these nations heavily rely on efficient transportation systems. Therefore, they invest in the development and improvement of transport infrastructure, such as railways and pipelines. Additionally, landlocked countries actively participate in regional and international trade agreements to reduce trade barriers and facilitate the movement of goods and services.

Landlocked countries are vulnerable to border conflicts and territorial disputes due to their geographic location. These conflicts can significantly impact their foreign policy decisions. To address this challenge, landlocked countries adopt diplomatic strategies to establish peaceful relations with neighboring countries and resolve disputes through dialogue and negotiation. They actively engage in multilateral cooperation and rely on international organizations to mediate and facilitate peaceful resolutions.

Development aid and assistance play a crucial role in supporting landlocked countries' development efforts and enhancing their foreign policy capabilities. These nations rely on foreign aid to improve their infrastructure, enhance their education and healthcare systems, and promote economic development. Development assistance also helps landlocked countries strengthen their diplomatic ties and establish international cooperation.

In conclusion, landlocked countries face unique challenges and limitations that require specific policy measures to attract foreign investment, promote export diversification, and reduce trade barriers. By adopting these measures, landlocked countries can overcome their geographic constraints, enhance their foreign policy capabilities, and achieve sustainable development.

Regional integration initiatives: Exploring the role of regional integration efforts in expanding market access for landlocked countries and enhancing their trade diversification.

Regional integration initiatives play a crucial role in expanding market access for landlocked countries and enhancing their trade diversification. These initiatives provide landlocked countries with a platform to overcome their geographic limitations and establish stronger economic ties with neighboring countries and the global market. This subchapter aims to explore the significance of regional integration efforts in addressing the specific challenges and limitations faced by landlocked countries.

Landlocked countries face numerous obstacles due to their lack of direct access to the sea. Limited trade routes and transportation infrastructure make it difficult for these countries to engage in international trade and diversify their economies. Regional integration initiatives, such as economic unions and free trade agreements, offer landlocked countries an opportunity to overcome these limitations by providing them with access to larger markets and facilitating the movement of goods and services.

Furthermore, regional integration initiatives also enable landlocked countries to reduce their dependence on neighboring countries for trade. By diversifying their trade partners, landlocked countries can mitigate the risks associated with relying on a single market and expand their export opportunities. This not only enhances their economic resilience but also strengthens their bargaining power in international trade negotiations.

In addition to expanding market access, regional integration initiatives also contribute to the overall development of landlocked countries. Through multilateral cooperation and collaboration, these initiatives promote the sharing of knowledge, resources, and best practices among member states. This allows landlocked countries to learn from the experiences of others and implement effective policies and strategies to overcome their unique challenges.

Moreover, regional integration initiatives play a crucial role in enhancing landlocked countries' foreign policy capabilities and diplomatic strategies. By forming regional alliances and establishing strong diplomatic relations, landlocked countries can effectively advocate for their interests and address security concerns. These initiatives also provide a platform for landlocked countries to participate in regional decision-making processes, thus influencing geopolitical dynamics and regional power balances.

In conclusion, regional integration initiatives offer landlocked countries a variety of opportunities to expand market access, diversify their trade partners, and overcome their unique limitations. By actively participating in these initiatives, landlocked countries can enhance their economic resilience, strengthen their diplomatic relations, and drive their overall development. It is imperative for diplomats and policymakers to recognize the importance of regional integration efforts and actively support and promote them in order to unlock the full potential of landlocked countries.

# Chapter 9: Security challenges: Assessing the unique security concerns faced by landlocked countries and their influence on foreign policy decisions.

Regional security dynamics: Examining the impact of regional conflicts and instability on landlocked countries' security and foreign policy choices.

Regional security dynamics play a crucial role in shaping the security and foreign policy choices of landlocked countries. These countries, surrounded by land and lacking direct access to the sea, face unique challenges and limitations that are exacerbated by regional conflicts and instability. This subchapter aims to examine the impact of regional conflicts and instability on the security and foreign policy choices of landlocked countries, providing valuable insights for diplomats and policymakers.

Landlocked countries, by virtue of their geographical location, are often more vulnerable to the spill-over effects of regional conflicts. Instability in neighboring countries can have far-reaching consequences on their security and foreign policy decisions. For instance, cross-border conflicts and territorial disputes can directly threaten the sovereignty and territorial integrity of landlocked nations, compelling them to adopt defensive measures and alliances to safeguard their interests.

The geopolitical landscape and regional power dynamics also significantly influence the foreign policy choices of landlocked countries. These countries have the potential to play a crucial role in regional alliances and conflicts due to their strategic location. Their participation in regional organizations and initiatives can be instrumental in shaping the overall balance of power in the region.

Furthermore, limited access to trade routes due to being landlocked imposes significant economic challenges on these countries. Regional conflicts and instability can further exacerbate these limitations, hindering their economic growth and resource management. In response, landlocked countries often adopt unique diplomatic strategies to establish international cooperation and relations, seeking alternative trade routes and diversifying their trade partners to reduce dependence on neighboring countries.

Efficient transport infrastructure, such as railways and pipelines, assumes paramount importance for landlocked countries' foreign policies. The development of robust transportation systems not only enhances their connectivity with international markets but also strengthens their bargaining power in regional alliances and negotiations.

In light of the increased vulnerability to border conflicts and territorial disputes, landlocked countries face complex security challenges. These concerns significantly influence their foreign policy decisions, as they seek to mitigate risks and ensure stability within their borders. Multilateral cooperation, facilitated through international organizations and agreements, plays a crucial role in assisting landlocked countries in overcoming their geographic constraints and addressing security challenges.

Foreign aid and assistance also play a pivotal role in supporting landlocked countries' development efforts and enhancing their foreign policy capabilities. Development projects, financial support, and technical expertise provided by external actors can help alleviate the limitations faced by landlocked countries and enable them to pursue their foreign policy objectives more effectively.

In conclusion, regional conflicts and instability have a profound impact on the security and foreign policy choices of landlocked countries. By recognizing and understanding these dynamics, diplomats and policymakers can better navigate the challenges faced by landlocked nations and work towards establishing sustainable and effective foreign policies that promote peace, security, and economic development.

Non-traditional security threats: Analyzing the challenges posed by non-traditional security issues, such as illicit trade, terrorism, and climate change, for landlocked countries.

Landlocked countries face a myriad of unique challenges and limitations that significantly impact their security and development. While the traditional security threats of military aggression and territorial disputes remain relevant, the rise of non-traditional security issues has added a new dimension to the vulnerabilities faced by these nations. This subchapter examines the specific challenges posed by non-traditional security threats, such as illicit trade, terrorism, and climate change, for landlocked countries.

One of the key challenges for landlocked countries is the issue of illicit trade. These nations often serve as transit points for smuggling activities due to their limited control over their borders and lack of direct access to trade routes. Illicit trade not only undermines the economy and hinders development efforts but also poses serious security risks, as it can fuel organized crime and terrorist activities.

Terrorism is another non-traditional security threat that landlocked countries must grapple with. These nations often find themselves vulnerable to terrorist infiltration and extremist ideologies due to their geographical location and limited security apparatus. The threat of terrorism not only undermines stability but also presents significant challenges for foreign policy decisions, as landlocked countries must balance security concerns with the need to foster international cooperation and trade relations.

Climate change poses yet another challenge for landlocked countries. These nations are particularly vulnerable to the adverse effects of climate change, such as droughts, floods, and changing weather patterns. These environmental challenges not only impact agricultural productivity and food security but also exacerbate resource scarcity and socio-economic disparities, leading to potential conflicts and security concerns.

Addressing these non-traditional security threats requires a comprehensive and multi-faceted approach. Landlocked countries must enhance their border control mechanisms to combat illicit trade and strengthen regional cooperation to tackle terrorism. Additionally, they need to prioritize climate change adaptation and mitigation strategies to build resilience and minimize the security risks associated with environmental challenges.

In conclusion, non-traditional security threats pose significant challenges for landlocked countries. Illicit trade, terrorism, and climate change not only impact the security and development of these nations but also influence their foreign policy decisions. By understanding and analyzing these challenges, landlocked countries can develop effective strategies and policies to overcome their unique limitations and ensure their sustainable development and security.

Chapter 10: Development aid and assistance: Exploring the role of foreign aid and assistance in supporting landlocked countries' development efforts and enhancing their foreign policy capabilities.

Aid dependency and its implications: Assessing the benefits and challenges associated with foreign aid for landlocked countries' development and diplomatic strategies.

Aid dependency and its implications: Assessing the benefits and challenges associated with foreign aid for landlocked countries' development and diplomatic strategies

In the realm of international development and diplomacy, landlocked countries face a unique set of challenges and limitations. Surrounded by land and lacking direct access to the sea, these nations grapple with a range of obstacles that impede their economic growth, resource management, and foreign policy objectives. One crucial aspect of overcoming these limitations is the role of foreign aid and assistance in supporting their development efforts and enhancing their diplomatic capabilities.

Foreign aid has long been recognized as a vital tool for addressing the specific challenges faced by landlocked countries. It provides them with the necessary financial resources to invest in infrastructure development, such as efficient transportation systems like railways and pipelines. By improving connectivity and reducing transportation costs, these investments can significantly enhance landlocked countries' foreign policy capabilities, opening up new trade routes and markets.

However, aid dependency can also have its drawbacks. While foreign aid can provide much-needed support, it can also foster a sense of reliance on external assistance. Landlocked countries must be cautious not to become overly dependent on aid, as this can hinder their long-term development and sovereignty. It is essential for these nations to strike a delicate balance between utilizing aid effectively and pursuing self-sufficiency through domestic resource mobilization and trade diversification.

Furthermore, foreign aid can also impact landlocked countries' diplomatic strategies. It can provide them with leverage and influence on the international stage, enabling them to establish partnerships and alliances that enhance their regional dynamics. Aid can also play a crucial role in addressing security concerns, as it can be directed towards strengthening border security and resolving territorial disputes, thus shaping foreign policy decisions.

Multilateral cooperation is another key aspect of aid for landlocked countries. International organizations and agreements provide these nations with a platform to engage with other countries facing similar challenges, share best practices, and collectively address their unique limitations. Through multilateral cooperation, landlocked countries can better advocate for their interests and influence the global agenda on issues that directly affect their development and diplomatic strategies.

In conclusion, foreign aid plays a critical role in supporting the development efforts and enhancing the diplomatic capabilities of landlocked countries. While aid dependency can pose challenges, when utilized effectively, aid can be a catalyst for economic growth, resource management, and regional cooperation. By carefully navigating the benefits and challenges associated with foreign aid, landlocked countries can overcome their unique limitations and establish themselves as active players in the global arena.

Capacity-building support: Investigating the role of development assistance in strengthening landlocked countries' institutions, infrastructure, and human resources for sustainable development.

Capacity-building support plays a crucial role in strengthening landlocked countries' institutions, infrastructure, and human resources for sustainable development. This subchapter aims to investigate the significance of development assistance in addressing the unique challenges faced by landlocked countries and enhancing their foreign policy capabilities.

Landlocked countries face specific limitations and challenges due to their geographic location. They lack direct access to major trade routes, making them heavily dependent on transit countries for their international trade. As a result, their economies and resource management are profoundly impacted by limited access to trade routes. This section will delve into the consequences of resource dependence and analyze its effects on the economy and resource management of landlocked countries.

To overcome these challenges, landlocked countries adopt unique foreign policy approaches to establish international cooperation and relations. Diplomatic strategies play a crucial role in mitigating the limitations imposed by geographic constraints. This subchapter will examine the diplomatic strategies adopted by landlocked countries to foster international cooperation and establish beneficial relationships with neighboring and transit countries.

The influence of landlocked countries on regional alliances, conflicts, and power dynamics is another important aspect to explore. Despite their geographic limitations, landlocked countries can significantly impact regional geopolitics and dynamics. This section will delve into the influence of landlocked countries on regional alliances, conflicts, and power dynamics and analyze how they navigate these complex relationships.

Efficient transport infrastructure, such as railways and pipelines, is vital for landlocked countries to overcome their geographic limitations. This subchapter will investigate the significance of efficient transportation systems for landlocked countries' foreign policies. It will explore how the development and improvement of transport infrastructure can enhance connectivity, trade, and cooperation with neighboring countries and beyond.

Border conflicts and territorial disputes pose increased vulnerabilities for landlocked countries. The impact of these conflicts on foreign policy decisions will be studied in this subchapter. It will analyze how landlocked countries navigate border disputes and the role of these conflicts in shaping their foreign policy decisions.

Multilateral cooperation plays a pivotal role in assisting landlocked countries in overcoming their geographic constraints. This section will analyze the role of international organizations and agreements in providing support and assistance to landlocked countries. It will explore how multilateral cooperation can enhance landlocked countries' development efforts and help them overcome the challenges they face.

Trade diversification is crucial for landlocked countries to reduce their dependence on neighboring countries. This subchapter will examine the strategies employed by landlocked countries to diversify their trade partners and expand their economic networks. It will analyze the impact of trade diversification on landlocked countries' foreign policies and their overall development efforts.

Security challenges are also unique concerns for landlocked countries. This section will assess the specific security concerns faced by landlocked countries and explore their influence on foreign policy decisions. It will delve into the strategies adopted by landlocked countries to address security challenges and ensure their national interests are protected.

Development aid and assistance play a crucial role in supporting landlocked countries' development efforts and enhancing their foreign policy capabilities. This subchapter will explore the role of foreign aid and assistance in strengthening landlocked countries' institutions, infrastructure, and human resources for sustainable development. It will analyze how development assistance can contribute to overcoming the unique challenges faced by landlocked countries and enhancing their capacity for effective foreign policymaking.

In conclusion, this subchapter aims to provide diplomats and those interested in landlocked countries with a comprehensive understanding of the role of development assistance in strengthening landlocked countries' institutions, infrastructure, and human resources for sustainable development. It explores the various challenges faced by landlocked countries and how capacity-building support can address these challenges and enhance their foreign policy capabilities.

Special Chapter about five landlocked countries: Bolivia, Paraguay, Uganda, Mongolia and Belarus

## Bolivia

Bolivia is one of the two landlocked countries in South America, the other being Paraguay. Being landlocked has presented Bolivia with a set of unique challenges and complexities over the years. Here are some specific difficulties faced by Bolivia due to its landlocked geography:

1. **Access to Sea Ports**: Being landlocked means Bolivia has no direct access to the ocean. This affects its trade dynamics, as it has to rely on neighboring countries, especially Chile and Peru, for port access. Bolivia has to negotiate terms, pay customs duties, and follow lengthy bureaucratic processes, leading to increased costs and time delays for its exports and imports.

2. **Historical Context**: Bolivia lost its coastline to Chile in the War of the Pacific (1879-1883). The loss of the Litoral Department, a coastal territory, has been a source of national grief and a point of contention in Bolivia's relationship with Chile. Though the International Court of Justice ruled in 2018 that Chile was not obligated to negotiate sovereign access to the Pacific Ocean for Bolivia, the historical loss remains a sensitive issue.

3. **Economic Impact**: The added costs of transporting goods to and from distant ports can make Bolivian goods less competitive in global markets. Moreover,

the potential for disruptions, such as strikes or political disagreements in transit countries, can further impede Bolivia's trade.

4. **Dependency on Neighboring Countries**: Bolivia's landlocked status makes it more dependent on the infrastructure, political stability, and policies of its neighbors. Any significant change in relations or internal affairs of these transit countries can affect Bolivia's trade routes and economic stability.

5. **Limited Maritime Training and Industry**: Direct access to the sea often leads to the development of maritime industries, training facilities, and expertise in naval matters. Being landlocked, Bolivia has limitations in this regard, though it does maintain a small naval presence on its lakes and rivers.

6. **Impact on Fisheries and Seafood Industry**: Direct access to the sea allows countries to have a vibrant fisheries sector. Bolivia doesn't have this advantage and hence relies on imports or freshwater fisheries for its seafood needs.

7. **Tourism Limitations**: Coastal areas often attract a significant amount of tourism due to beaches, marine activities, and related attractions. Bolivia misses out on this kind of tourism, although it compensates with other forms of tourism, like cultural, historical, and ecological tourism, given its rich indigenous heritage and diverse ecosystems.

8. **Limited Access to Maritime Resources**: Beyond fisheries, the oceans offer a range of resources, from oil and gas deposits to potential sources of renewable

energy like tidal and wave energy. Bolivia doesn't have direct access to these potential resources.

It's worth noting, however, that while being landlocked poses challenges, Bolivia has unique strengths and assets, such as its rich cultural heritage, vast mineral resources (like lithium), and biodiversity, which offer significant opportunities for development and growth.

## Paraguay

Paraguay, along with Bolivia, is one of the two landlocked countries in South America. Its landlocked status has shaped its historical, economic, and geopolitical circumstances in various ways. Here are some of the specific difficulties faced by Paraguay due to its landlocked geography:

1. **Access to Sea Ports**: Without direct access to the ocean, Paraguay relies on the river systems, particularly the Paraná and Paraguay Rivers, for its exports and imports. While these rivers are navigable and crucial for the country's trade, they flow through several countries before reaching the Atlantic Ocean. This dependency means Paraguay has to negotiate terms and navigate the regulations of other nations.

2. **Economic Impact**: The absence of a coastline increases the costs of trade. Goods need to be transported over longer distances, often passing through other countries, leading to additional tariffs, fees, and potential delays. This can make Paraguayan products less competitive on the global market.

3. **Dependency on Neighboring Countries**: Relying on ports in Argentina or Brazil for exports and imports makes Paraguay somewhat dependent on the policies, infrastructure, and political stability of these countries. Any disruptions, such as labor strikes or geopolitical tensions, can hamper Paraguay's trade.

4. **Limited Maritime Training and Industry**: While Paraguay has developed expertise related to river navigation and has a merchant marine fleet that operates on its rivers, the country doesn't have industries associated with deep-sea navigation, shipbuilding, or oceanic exploration.

5. **Tourism Limitations**: Coastal areas tend to attract tourists due to beaches and marine activities. Paraguay lacks seaside tourism potential but has focused on other forms of tourism, such as ecotourism and cultural attractions.

6. **Limited Access to Maritime Resources**: Oceans offer resources, such as oil, gas, and other minerals. Being landlocked, Paraguay can't directly access these resources from oceanic regions.

7. **Geopolitical Limitations**: Paraguay's landlocked geography means it must maintain good diplomatic relations with its neighbors, especially Argentina and Brazil, to ensure smooth trade routes. This can sometimes limit its foreign policy choices.

8. **Environmental and Infrastructure Concerns**: The heavy reliance on river systems makes Paraguay vulnerable to environmental changes. Fluctuations in river levels, sedimentation, or pollution can affect

navigation and trade. Additionally, the country needs to invest in infrastructure to ensure its rivers remain navigable and to maintain efficient transport links to sea ports in neighboring countries.

However, being landlocked also pushes a country to develop unique solutions and strategies. For instance, Paraguay has utilized its river systems effectively for trade. The country has also invested in its hydroelectric sector, with the Itaipú Dam being a prime example of leveraging its geographical strengths. This dam, jointly operated with Brazil, is one of the largest hydroelectric facilities in the world, showcasing how Paraguay has turned some of its geographical challenges into opportunities.

## Uganda

Uganda, situated in East Africa, is landlocked and surrounded by Kenya, Tanzania, Rwanda, South Sudan, and the Democratic Republic of the Congo. Being landlocked has posed both historical and contemporary challenges for Uganda. Here are some specific difficulties faced by the country due to its lack of direct access to the coast:

1. **Access to Sea Ports**: Uganda relies heavily on the Kenyan port of Mombasa and the Tanzanian port of Dar es Salaam for its imports and exports. The long overland journey from these ports to Uganda adds to the time and cost of transportation.
2. **Increased Trade Costs**: The additional distance goods must travel from sea ports, combined with potential

delays at border crossings, can lead to higher costs for both imports and exports. This makes Ugandan products less competitive in international markets and increases the cost of imported goods for Ugandan consumers.

3. **Dependency on Transit Countries**: Uganda's trade is largely dependent on the infrastructure, policies, and political stability of its neighboring countries, especially Kenya and Tanzania. Disruptions, such as infrastructure issues, bureaucratic delays, or political tensions in these transit countries, can have significant impacts on Ugandan trade.

4. **Transportation Challenges**: The road and rail networks connecting Uganda to coastal ports have historically faced challenges related to maintenance, capacity, and efficiency. While there have been investments and improvements, transport inefficiencies continue to pose challenges.

5. **Vulnerability to Economic Shocks**: Any disruption in the major transit routes, whether due to political issues, natural disasters, or other factors, can lead to significant economic repercussions for Uganda. This makes the country more vulnerable to external shocks.

6. **Limited Maritime Sector Development**: Being landlocked, Uganda lacks opportunities related to maritime industries such as shipbuilding, deep-sea fishing, or oceanic exploration.

7. **Geopolitical Considerations**: Being dependent on neighboring countries for trade access can sometimes influence Uganda's foreign policy decisions, as

maintaining good relations with these nations becomes crucial for economic reasons.

8. **Tourism Limitations**: While Uganda has a rich offering in terms of wildlife, cultural tourism, and natural beauty, it doesn't benefit from coastal or marine tourism, which can be significant revenue earners for countries.

9. **Economic Diversification Challenges**: Access to the sea can provide countries with opportunities for economic diversification, such as maritime trade, fisheries, and offshore energy production. Uganda's landlocked status means it doesn't have direct access to these opportunities.

However, it's important to note that while being landlocked presents challenges, Uganda has several strengths and assets. The country is endowed with fertile land, freshwater resources, diverse ecosystems, and significant mineral deposits. Over the years, Uganda has also tried to leverage regional integration mechanisms, such as the East African Community (EAC), to mitigate some of the challenges of its landlocked status and improve trade and transportation links with its neighbors.

## Mongolia

Mongolia is unique not only because it's landlocked, but also due to its location between two of the world's major powers: Russia and China. This geographic situation has historically and contemporaneously influenced Mongolia's economic, political, and strategic dynamics. Here are some specific difficulties faced by Mongolia owing to its landlocked status:

1. **Access to Ports**: Mongolia depends on transit routes through Russia and China to access seaports for its international trade. This reliance adds to the costs, time, and logistical complexities of transportation.
2. **Increased Trade Costs**: Transporting goods over long overland routes and across international borders adds to the expenses for Mongolian exports and imports. Such costs can impact the competitiveness of Mongolian products on the international market and increase the price of imported goods for domestic consumers.
3. **Dependency on Neighboring Countries**: Mongolia's trade largely hinges on the infrastructure, political stability, and policies of Russia and China. Disruptions in these countries or changes in their policies can significantly influence Mongolian trade. For instance, a strained relationship with either neighbor or internal issues within these countries can create bottlenecks for Mongolian exports and imports.
4. **Transportation Infrastructure**: While Mongolia has been investing in its transportation infrastructure, the vastness of the country combined with its challenging terrains and extreme climate makes the development and maintenance of roads and railways demanding.
5. **Geopolitical Challenges**: Being sandwiched between Russia and China means Mongolia often has to balance its relationships with both powers. This positioning can be challenging, especially when geopolitical tensions arise between its two neighbors.
6. **Economic Diversification Issues**: Mongolia's

economy is heavily dependent on mining, especially coal and copper. Access to a broader range of economic activities associated with maritime access, such as shipping or fisheries, is not available to Mongolia.

7.  **Vulnerability to Economic Shocks**: With primary trade routes going through just two countries, Mongolia is more susceptible to external economic shocks. If one of its neighbors experiences economic downturns or decides to change trade policies, it can have outsized effects on the Mongolian economy.

8.  **Limited Direct Foreign Market Access**: Being landlocked and surrounded by only two countries restricts Mongolia's direct access to diverse foreign markets. This limitation can affect foreign investments and partnerships.

9.  **Cultural and Touristic Impacts**: While Mongolia has a rich cultural heritage and vast scenic beauty, the absence of sea-related tourism limits the spectrum of its touristic offerings.

However, it's essential to recognize that Mongolia's strategic location also provides opportunities. For instance, initiatives like China's Belt and Road Initiative (BRI) can potentially boost Mongolia's connectivity and trade prospects. Mongolia's vast mineral resources, combined with its traditional nomadic culture and breathtaking landscapes, offer unique strengths that can be leveraged for economic and cultural benefits.

Belarus

Belarus, located in Eastern Europe, is landlocked and bordered by Russia, Ukraine, Poland, Lithuania, and Latvia. While it is situated in a geopolitically significant location, its landlocked status does present challenges. Here are some of the specific difficulties faced by Belarus because of its lack of direct access to the sea:

1. **Access to Ports**: Belarus is reliant on transit routes through neighboring countries to access seaports for its international trade, primarily through the Baltic Sea ports of Lithuania and Latvia. Dependence on these transit routes can add logistical complexities and costs.

2. **Increased Trade Costs**: Overland transportation can be more expensive than sea freight. Having to move goods through neighboring countries can lead to additional transit fees, potential delays at borders, and higher transportation costs, which can impact the competitiveness of Belarusian products.

3. **Geopolitical Vulnerabilities**: Belarus's trade routes are influenced by its political relations with neighboring countries. A strained relationship with any of its neighbors can impact its trade dynamics. The country's close ties with Russia and its more complex relationship with the European Union (EU) countries can influence its economic decisions and trade routes.

4. **Dependency on Transit Countries**: For Belarus, relying on neighboring countries' infrastructure and policies can pose challenges. Disruptions in these transit routes, whether due to political issues, infrastructure breakdowns, or other factors, can affect

the steady flow of goods in and out of Belarus.

5. **Economic Diversification Challenges**: Being landlocked can limit opportunities for certain industries, such as maritime or fisheries. While Belarus has a robust industrial base, its landlocked status can restrict the spectrum of economic activities available.

6. **Energy Security Concerns**: Belarus heavily depends on Russia for its energy supplies, especially oil and gas. This dependency is not solely because of its landlocked status but is exacerbated by it, given the lack of direct access to alternative maritime oil and gas routes.

7. **Foreign Policy Constraints**: Being sandwiched between the European Union and Russia, Belarus often finds itself balancing its relationships. Its landlocked geography further emphasizes the need to maintain stable relations with neighboring countries to ensure open trade routes.

8. **Tourism Limitations**: While Belarus offers a rich cultural and historical heritage, it lacks sea-related tourism opportunities, which can be significant attractions for many nations.

However, it's worth noting that Belarus has tried to leverage its geographical position as a transit country between the EU and Russia. It's part of the Eurasian Economic Union (EAEU), which aims to boost economic ties between member countries. Moreover, its location offers potential as a logistical hub, and it has tried to position itself as such, especially with projects like the Great Stone Industrial Park, a Belarus-China joint initiative.

www.ingramcontent.com/pod-product-compliance
Lightning Source LLC
Chambersburg PA
CBHW051315160726
47994CB00003B/1463